101 ANG
CHALLENGE

WELCOME

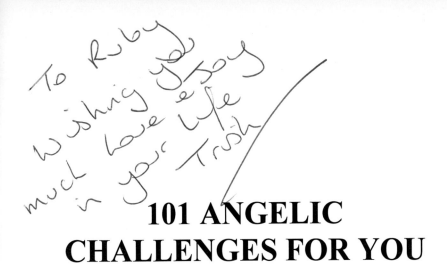

To Ruby
Wishing you
much love & Joy
in your life
Trish

101 ANGELIC
CHALLENGES FOR YOU

Patricia A. Watson

First published in 2010 by:
P A Watson

[ISBN: 978-0-9566617-0-8]

Printed and bound in Great Britain by:
Proprint, Remus House Coltsfoot Drive,
Woodston, Peterborough, PE2 9JX

MY INTRODUCTION

I am the last person to believe that I would be fortunate enough to be gifted with a book full of channelings from the Angelic Kingdom, but indeed I have, and as I have been inspired hearing their words, I hope you will also be inspired as you read the same words. Their wish is that you will read one of their challenges as often as possible; whichever one you turn to will be the one fitting for you to dwell on for that day.

I have been blessed in the past few years to be able to follow my own path. As so many of you will know, that is not always easy. An expression I use is 'Life got in the way'- lots of work, lots of responsibilities, and not enough time to do the things I wanted to. But then things started to change; more time seemed available for my own interests. After training I became a Usui Reiki Master (I am not its master, but it is the Master of me). I also trained as a Person Centered Counsellor of Carl Rogers' theories. These and other challenges all led me back to the spiritual path I had started on in my youth.

I have been inspired by many wonderful authors of Angelic and Spiritual books. They have encouraged me to try for myself and to connect to the Angels. It took much time and patience (something that was hard for me to learn) but once it started to work, there was no going back...that is, except for my own self doubt, which I still have to work on, but then I do have wonderful help.

When I asked why I had been chosen, like so many others have, to put their words forward, this was part of their reply:
'We firstly chose yourself, not only because of your willingness to listen to us, but also your past lives and your

utmost belief in us. We wish to get through to people we would not normally get through to, mainly to reach a wider audience; because you are so down to earth, but see things from a loving but basic perspective, and we feel this way we may reach even more people, because, our beloved, everyone really does need to start working so hard for your Earth, for it and yourself to survive'.

So with such love and belief handed to me I feel I have no alternative but to at least attempt to offer you their words of love and encouragement for a more fulfilling life.

I hope you enjoy their words, and if you cannot take on board all that is offered to you, then may at least a seed be set and grow within and blossom when your time is right.

The group of Angels I have been working with are five in number who have been studying our life here on Earth a very long time, and say that with 'just by a few simple changes' in what we are doing, our lives can change considerably.

I give thanks to Sheila for all her hard work and support, to my Reiki share group, who have such belief in me, and lastly, but could never be least, my husband John, for loving football so much; it gave me time and space to pursue my dreams.

I send love to you all, and remember you are privileged as indeed I am, to receive love and guidance from our Angels.

Trish

A Message to Each and Every One of You

From the Five Golden Angels

Lleuvbri Petrall Donuni

Maruna and Orbrial

The energy is changing so quickly there on Earth, and you must change with it for the human race and the Earth to survive.

In our book to you we would like to say that no one needs all of the 101 Angelic Challenges, but you all need some of them.

Don't look for each one to be more complicated than it is. The simpler you make each one, the more you will succeed. You are only asked to do your own personal best, and then move on to the next one of your choice.

There is no particular order to read this Angelic book. Choose a number or page at random. It will be the right one for you on that day.

We wish you Joy, Peace, Love and Healing for the life you have chosen there on Earth, and never forget we walk with you always, and that you are never alone, and that you are always surrounded by our love.

CHALLENGE 1

Feelings that are all confused within you will all eventually
be sorted out.

But there are so many feelings within you that do not need
sorting out at all. The only thing that is needed is confidence
to be applied to them, which you seem to have one minute,
then let go the next. Please learn to give yourself the
confidence, as you so freely give to others.

You have so many repeat lessons to learn, but it is what you
requested, and life on Earth is such a short time, compared
with infinity, and in your heart you know this to be true.

It is just so difficult in this world of yours, and as you and
others work so hard to improve the light, love and healing
within your world, so are others working the opposite way.
They are working harder than ever now, for it is difficult for
them to understand how something so light and loving can
move Mountains, while it takes them so long to disrupt a
pebble.

We can feel you questioning that statement, but you cannot
see from this side the whole of what is going on. We wish
you to know that the Light, Love and Healing are being sent
from you to others and the Earth is working.

Love with many thanks is being sent to all those working so
hard. We are proud to walk with you all.

CHALLENGE 2

We accept everything you are. It is called unconditional love, which you seem to give to everyone but yourself. You seem to set yourself such high standards.

We think the expression you would use is 'moving the goal posts'. Every time you succeed with a challenge, action or deed, instead of saying well done to yourself, you move your own goal posts. Be as you are to others; be also kinder to yourself, challenging, yes, but also kinder.

No one here or on Earth thinks it's easy being a human there on Earth at this time, so please be kinder and love yourself more.

These words are for all those on the Light path. Please watch for our sharing moments that we have with you all on Earth.

We wish you and yours Peace, Love, Light, Wisdom and Healing, and to those that you meet on life's path.

CHALLENGE 3

You all must learn on Earth to listen to your heart, your senses, and the small voice within. Learn to have confidence in what you quietly hear. Make your own voice more quietly spoken, so you may hear the peace above it.

Don't always do the safe things in life, but the things you really want to do. You may not always try the right path to start with, but if you ask that it be for the greater and higher good of all, then you will soon see the right path to take. It just may lead you to far more sunshine that you ever thought possible. You must start to listen with the heart and not the mind.

Far too many people and situations are getting left abandoned, and that in turn is creating more problems that you and others should never have to deal with. Nothing is irreversible. Just stop, look and listen. Try not to see through hurt, cynical eyes, but through veils of love. Even the smallest thought of love will help, and that will quickly grow, for more and more help and love is being given to your world and its people within it.

These teaspoons of messages and love are a good measure of what we mean, as you and others will find out as time goes by.

You are not expected to change the world on your own. You are not expected to worry continually about the state of things. Just being 'aware' is the first stage, then everything else will follow. The more joy you find the more will follow. Believe us. There is joy in all you see, hear and feel, yes, even at this time, which we know you will find difficult to believe.

We are always with you, giving love, help, guidance and support; our love enfolds you while you sleep.

CHALLENGE 4

Your precious world, with all its people, animals, birds, fish, trees, plants, mountains, caves, every type of matter known on your Earth, is crying out to its God for Help.

What you all don't seem to realize, you are all asking for the same things. It is just being asked for in so many different ways, and do you know, if you all got to know each other just that little bit better, you wouldn't have to be asking your maker for help.

Love, guidance, protection and help are within each and every one of you. A little more respect and kindness for each other would go such a long way to healing that which is in dire need of healing.

Yes we know there seem to be so many dark forces around, but believe us, their power is nothing in comparison to the power all you other wonderful souls have. You wonderful souls, that feel so battered and bruised and at times lost.

We implore you to cast aside your negativity; surround yourself with love and protection and just see the great changes start to happen, not just in your life, but those you love and work with. Then the many that are already working on their own will join you in spirit, to surge forward in an almighty swell of light that will create a greater good for All mankind.

Yes time is short, but never too short for the betterment of your troubled Earth.

You are and always will be our precious child.

CHALLENGE 5

Peace, Love, Light and Healing. These words that you or some one around you says often. These words are now said to you.
We wish you all Peace, Love, Light and Healing and also to all those you love.

As the time moves on, the stars will once again shine brightly for all those who believe in the above words. So much confirmation of 'our' home is all around you, as we await your safe return to your true home.

Please share this information with as many people as possible. You don't have to convince anyone. Just tell them as it is, then they will find their own path in their own time, which will be much sooner than any of you thought possible.

May your spirit be lighter. May you laugh more, hurt less. Look for the joy that is all around you. That alone will dissolve a lot of negativity that is within. For as you know, everything starts from within, everything.

Your God hears and sees all. We are his servants, and Love you unconditionally.

CHALLENGE 6

Love comes in many shapes, sizes and colours, but whatever one tries to do in life, if it is not done with Love, goodness, depth and lasting strength, and for the greater good of all men, then whatever is being attempted will not last.

This may seem hard for you to understand at this time, with so many things being done, and seemingly achieved, without love, but you don't see the whole picture. We have to say, we don't always either, but we do see more than yourself.

We have such faith, belief and love for our Mother and Father God, who has never, ever let any of his children down.

Whatever happens in your world, you will always return to your home here, where you will be surrounded by so much love, learning, beauty and so many soul partners, and it may not be until you look back, that you will realize how shallow some things were, and that which wasn't done with 'love' will just falter and fail.

What we ask of our Earth sisters and brothers is that you trust us, even if it's only a fraction of our trust and love in you. For we will be delighted at the happiness that will take place on your planet Earth.

Please stay strong in your belief, have courage in despair, share your love and smiles with as many people as possible.

Always remember, you are never alone. We walk with you and love you at all times.

CHALLENGE 7

Well be, those of you that look for the light and love, for it is all around you and your loved ones.

But then not all are open or willing to see the love and energy that is there waiting for them. And as we here sit back and wait for those people to change, so you on Earth must do likewise.

Try to live by what you believe in; try to love your neighbour, along with all those you meet on life's path. That is all that is asked of you. If you cannot do this, and follow through that love, there is no disgrace, just move on with your life, but not before wrapping light and love, with your mind's eye, around those you are leaving. That alone will be enough to water the seed of love in your neighbour's mind.

It is not possible for all to progress at the same rate or speed. Each of you is there on Earth to learn different things.

It may all seem confusing, the many different cultures, conflicts and problems on your Earth. We ask that you all stand strong in your faith, belief and spirituality, to be the guiding light that will be needed for all, in times to come.

You are very much loved, and not on your own, ever.

CHALLENGE 8

Listen to your heart, and whatever rings true at the time. Then that is the truth, your truth. It belongs to you. Have courage to believe in it and when necessary act upon it.

But if you are never really sure, wait. Don't act on a whim or guess. It will be that the time is just not quite right, and there could be bigger and better delights around the corner, and our corner could be years away, but it will be better to wait for the right 'happening' than wasting years upon the wrong path, as indeed, you all seem to do at some time or other. So try and have more belief and trust in yourself.

The energy around you all is changing, affecting the air around you. So please make sure you can be in as clean air as possible. You need space to connect to the changing energy, so that we can work in peace and quiet with you.

We are always at your side, walking with you, with our love.

CHALLENGE 9

It is with difficulty that you try to hear, sense and touch the unknown. It is not you alone that have these problems, but many others also. So please don't get down hearted if you don't progress how you think you should, because we tell you, our dear heart, your progression is on track, and we know you don't feel that you are moving fast, quickly or well enough, but all of a sudden you will look back and wonder how you got so far, without even knowing.

Yes you are right to say there is so much to learn, but what you have previously learnt on your spiritual path is at this time hidden from you. It will shortly come back to you, with all you have experienced before. It will be with disbelief to begin with, and then the light and truth will dawn. This will not only be for yourself, but others that you know also, and some people that you will be surprised about. Yes it is a very exciting time for you in many ways, not only spiritually, but the many Earth things that are to change or to come. They are right here waiting.

It is with love, light and guidance that we remain with you and those that you share your love and light with.

CHALLENGE 10

It is with love and uncertainty that you approach the forthcoming New Year. Time seems to be of great importance to you all on planet Earth. It is only when you return home again, that time will have no hold on you. But while you live your life on Earth, going through all your learning and lessons, it is understandable that you have a time schedule.

Your Earth is one of the greatest challenges you will ever have to face in your evolution, and like many others there on Earth, you have been there many times before, but as many of you know or sense, this time has many similarities to the Atlantis time.

As the Earth is going through many changes with energy, love and power, so is your own being going through many changes. So please don't get discouraged with yourself, when you don't cope well under adversity, or with not always doing or being what you would like to do or be.

You are coping well under such adversity and please let others know that they too are doing well. Encourage them with help and love, as we too try to encourage you with help and love, but as others may not always listen to you, you my child don't always listen to us.

As you love others, so we love you, with an even greater love, for we don't have all your negativity to deal with.

So we ask that you keep smiling, keep loving and keep believing. May your light shine not only for yourself but others as well.

CHALLENGE 11

As your New Year dawns, already many of you have proof of the changing energy there on Earth. More and more people will come to you and to others, and will want to learn, share and move forward with you and this new energy.

The wonders that are to come are such a delight, not just for you to see, but to see the joy in others will be just as great for you, and of course, your joy will be our joy.

We are all too aware that this can be very fragile, as darkness at times can become very thick, but stand firm, reassure one another, protect yourself with light and the purple pyramid, and never doubt that we are always with you.

Our messages are the pure truth, and to some will be very simple, even too simple, and that is what they will remain for quite some time, for we don't want there to be any misunderstanding in what we are saying.

Love, as you are loved. Never beat yourself up for not doing as well as you think you should. Just do your best. Nothing more will ever be expected of you, for to work at all, within all your negative energy on Earth, is quite remarkable.

CHALLENGE 12

To remove clutter from one's mind and body leaves room for more love and goodness to enter, and although this has been said by so many Feng Shui experts, it has also been said by so many of you in your everyday life.

Sometimes we would wish that you listened to your own words of wisdom far more closely and carefully, for this is so true from many factors and points of view.

If you clear out of your home that which is not needed, from cupboards, wardrobes, drawers and your office, of old papers, jottings, pens never used, we would be able to reach you so much quicker. The energy would be clearer, the dust not as great. Light would be able to shine to you.

Then do the same with your body, clear out all negativity, all worries, all crossness, all thoughts you are holding on to that do not nourish the soul. Never harbour resentment, jealousy and anger. Be strong and release as much as possible; it only ties you down.

It is time to fly. Be light (as in carrying heavy loads), so our Light may be with you and that we may be able to work together more. We will have such a wonderful time together.

As we tell you all the time, we will help you. Just ask. You are never alone and you are very much loved.

CHALLENGE 13

Courage: courage to be quiet and not argue, courage to remain silent and not hurt others, courage to speak one's own truth, courage to apologise, courage to smile at a stranger, courage to speak to a lonely person.

Courage comes in so many shapes and sizes, depth and quietness. But courage is what all 'light' people have and in this time of great change you will be helped more and more for your courage to grow, change and move forward, which in turn will encourage those around you to do likewise, just as you are encouraged to move forward, from those people around you.

The great quiet movement of light, love, healing and wisdom is gathering pace and volume, much more than any of you realize. Each and every one of you, continue all your works.

Go in Peace and with our love and protection.

CHALLENGE 14

As you wait for the next stage or chapter of your life, so we here watch with love and guidance, knowing some choices are so difficult for you to make. Please understand, there are really no bad or wrong choices. The only thing that would be wrong is if you stayed in a decision, knowing it wasn't the right one for you, because you are assigning pain and darkness to yourself.

Which, yes, is a learning curve, but wouldn't it be so much better to do your learning in light and love?

We always remain surprised how many of you choose the longest darkest road, but of course it isn't that long and dark, compared with infinity and you will have much joy in the light, in times to come.

We ask that you always remember, when you are in that darkness, we are always by your side, waiting to help you move into the light, but of course we cannot lead you there without you asking and giving permission to us. We also have to say, sometimes, our beloved ones, you don't want to listen to any one but yourselves. Try to be calm and still, listen to within.

Our love, as always, walks with you.

CHALLENGE 15

For a rose to come into flower, it will start as such a small bud, and slowly with the sun and rain, then the added warmth, so it will bloom.

Each and every rose is so different, even those on the same bush or tree, the colour, the texture, volume and size, but each and every one is so beautiful in its own way, it would be so hard to choose the most 'correct' one.

So it is with all the 'light' people on Earth. Each and every one of you is so different, but in no way does that mean that some of you are right and others wrong in their approach to life. Some of you have learnt so much in your previous lives; others amongst you have taken on a heavy load in this life, but all of you in your own way are still doing the same job, for our beloved Father & Mother God.

So we ask that you do not look for the difference amongst your fellow workers, but the similarities, and never think what you are doing is insignificant. Compared to someone you may be observing, each and every task you all do is so important. All that is ever asked of you is that you do your best, in all that you do.

As you strive to achieve this, we ask that you always ask and work in the Light. Try not to absorb or study darkness for too long. Yes we know you cannot ignore it, for to pretend it isn't there would be wrong, but to study it or remain in negativity too long weakens your Light.

As always we will be there with you. Never think you are alone, although we know it can be a lonely path for you at times. You are surrounded by Love, Light and Healing. Go with our love.

CHALLENGE 16

Step in to your own power.

This message is for all people on the Light path. You seem to work so hard in your own way, but it seems to be mainly for the good of others.

It now gets very close to the time for stepping into your own light and power. This doesn't mean control of others, for you all know, that is not the Light way. By stepping into your own power, all you ask for others, and they receive, start to ask for yourself. It is time to move forward with your work and deeds here on Earth. The next stage of your work here on Earth is now.

There are many people that this message is for, and they will know as soon as they read or hear these words. For others they may seem a little strange at this moment, but because you are hearing them, means your time is just around the corner.

All we ask is that you have faith in your belief and inner feelings, of right and wrong, of light and darkness. Don't be afraid of people with so called power. If you sense what they are doing is wrong, have faith in yourself and ask for help with (or for) those people. For we are here to work not only with you, but for you also.

You have, as always, our unconditional love and protection.

CHALLENGE 17

In this world called Earth, in case you didn't know, is the hardest school of learning that there is, anywhere in the galaxy.

It is only with working with you and others as a guide here on Earth, that I can say with hand on your heart, you are all so brave to repeat your many lives here. You all will be our Mother and Fathers God's special children, when you return home.

There are many that don't in the end manage to complete or carry out their intended life span, and some of you will know who we mean by this. We ask you not to judge others for their weakness or failings. There could be many reasons for this, and it's only on your return home that you will discover many, many reasons why things have happened here on Earth, as they have.

And who is to say what failure is and what success is. Only your soul and your Mother and Father God know that, and they would never criticize anything or anyone.

For how can you know any other person's life plan, when you cannot even understand your own, or those you love?

There is something we feel we should add here. If there is any one person that disturbs you, or you find in your heart hard to accept them, there is no wrong in that. Just try if possible to surround them in love. Yes you can do this with so called world leaders as well. Just surround them in love, and then turn away. You do not need them in your life. By doing this you will help them, and others near them, much more than you will ever know.

We here send you our undying love, protection, healing and light, not only on this day, but tomorrow and always.

CHALLENGE 18

Peace, Love, Light and Healing, oh to have those four wonders in your life. Not easy to achieve we know, but it is possible to have some and sometimes you can have all in your life, sometimes fleetingly, sometimes for longer, and sometimes, each is there waiting for you, very quietly, for you to take up any or all of these wonders, but more often than not you are so busy of mind with things that don't belong to you, that you miss these golden wonders.

The more you allow these wonders into your life, the more you will be able to receive them. For you will come to understand that although it is good and rightful to help or support others, your first priority always is to yourself, that is in all things, learning, caring, loving and cleanliness. These should all be done for yourself first and foremost, and the space or time you allow yourself, allow others also. For as no two, three or more plants grow in unison, neither do you all, and that is the beauty and wonder of you all.

So we ask you give yourself time and space to receive the above, and also to receive our love and devotion that is ALWAYS waiting for you.

We wish you all to know that each and every one is so very special and unique; to be master and control of yourself is far harder than trying to take charge of others.

CHALLENGE 19

As you try to sooth others, so you will be soothed.

Life is a circle, but it just doesn't include this lifetime, and that is where things get complicated and confusing to all you light souls there on Earth.

What is also hard for you to work out, is why at times your life seems more difficult than what you would wish for, or feels fair. But please believe us when we say, it is not a punishment from our Father and Mother God, but through your own choice.

When you were safe and so loved here at home, through your own love, you chose not only to go to Earth, the hardest of all schools, but chose many difficulties to overcome.

So please remember, when you feel despair and loneliness, please call on us, and we will petition for your release of pain. As for loneliness, that is always a state of mind, as we are always, for now and forever, with you, loving you, as you should love yourself.

CHALLENGE 20

The beauty of your heart only matches the beauty of your soul.

In your confusing world, the face, the figure, a person's clothes, money and standing, seem to make up a beauty that appeals to so many of you on Earth. In very rare circumstances these things may all come together, but we implore you all to just look a little deeper into the person.

We ask that you work, and continue to work with your heart and soul, and as we ask you to look for your own truth, in whatever you read about, see or hear, we ask the same rules apply when looking and meeting new people in your life, for like so many things, you may not see the truth straight away.

By working with your soul and heart on Earth, you will naturally become more beautiful in the beholder's eyes, or the ones that matter that is.

This also means us, and to us, you are very beautiful. Go forward with our love surrounding you.

CHALLENGE 21

The lotus flower has long been a symbol for love and knowledge. It can sit on top of your crown chakra and petal by petal it can be opened to let in more light, love, knowledge and wisdom to your mind.

We believe all that are listening or reading this piece of information are ready for all that is being handed down to you. We are only too happy to share all our knowledge and love with you, but we also know that if you receive more than a 'tea spoon' at a time, it may startle you or make you unsure, not only of yourself, but the path you are on, and beloved ones, that is the last thing we wish to do to you all.

As your confidence grows in all Light matters, so shall more information be handed to you. The speed of your knowledge and learning will greatly surprise you.

So never think you are moving too slow, or not trusted with more Light matters. It is we, your protectors, who are shielding you.

Never fear anything, our beloved ones. You are about to 'fly', never to crash, only to soar higher and higher.

Go with love, not only from us, but also from your Mother and Father God.

CHALLENGE 22

Your brothers and sisters and all your soul family, who await you at home, can also be called upon to help you, while you are there on Earth.

We often speak to you of our love and that we always walk with you, that you are never alone, which is so true. But for some, this is hard to understand or absorb.

So if you wish, you can also call on your brothers or sisters, who will also bring love, help and assistance to you.

Here at home all anyone wants to do is give help, assistance and strength to all that ask or require it. This is especially true in the coming times.

Which brings us to implore all that work for love and light there on Earth, please continue to do so, for each prayer and good deed manifests a hundred fold, which gives more light to all on Earth.

As you give, so shall you receive.

Love and Grace surround you.

CHALLENGE 23

Music, sounds, laughter, loving words, these all uplift the soul and heart. Music can carry you to the other end of the Earth, not only of memories of this life, but many before.

Not that you will remember that so much. A smile will come to your lips and love will surround your heart.

We ask each and every one of you to give time to yourself, be it with music, the sound of a bubbling stream, or birds singing to one another, dogs chasing and barking happily. Maybe your own joy is to read poetic words that someone has lovingly put together.

Whatever uplifts your heart and soul, always find time for yourself to enjoy these joys. It will help to sustain you through difficulties that are all part of life on Earth. You may even find that some difficulties are not quite as bad as they used to be.

Love yourself as we love you. We promise you more joy in your life by doing so.

CHALLENGE 24

You have so many lessons to learn there on Earth, but at times you tend to forget the many lessons you have already learnt. Each lesson, until it is learnt or dealt with in your correct way will keep reappearing. And that could be the second or hundredth time of repeating itself, but you will suddenly know the right thing for 'You' to do, with that particular problem or situation.

It is then we ask that you hold onto your belief and confidence to do the right thing for 'You'.
No two people are the same. You are here on your own path, and your 'right' is yours alone.
What others feel and think is right about your problem or situation, does not have to be the same as what you think. As indeed the same applies the other way round; when your friend has a problem, you may not agree with them.

You each should follow your own instinct; this in the long run will enable your learning to be shorter, as your problems and situations will be solved more quickly by each of you following your own path.

We ask that you do not control others by thought or deed, as you should not be controlled by thought or deed of others. You are indeed a beloved child of our Mother & Father God, so unique, so loved, so beautiful; go forward in your own light and confidence.

CHALLENGE 25

This fragile Earth of yours is going through so many changes right now, as indeed it always has gone through many changes.

Your Earth has been abused by all the men and women that live upon it, some times in ignorance, some times knowingly, then left the problems for the next generation to put right.

The time has now come that many decisions have to be made on how you continue your life on Earth, because the Earth's patience with man's destruction of its very balance is near its end.

Taxes and money cannot put right the situation, but if everyone just changes their own life a little, with thought, with love, and healing for your planet, these thoughts and deeds also directed to your fellow man, then you will all see great changes for the better.
It will all happen very quickly. You just have to all work together on this, and as you know, that will be the main difficulty -'working together'

There are those that are already doing this. They are blessed, helped and loved even more. We wait with the same help and love for all those searching for a way to help.
Your light shines brightly, helping all, your intent shining forth.

Our love and we, as always, walk with you and yours.

CHALLENGE 26

We speak to you and others all the time about love and light and these being the most important things on Earth, and how it can change so many things, starting of course with yourselves.

We are not blind or deaf to all the horrors that are happening on your Earth. If it is not happening to you personally, it will be to people or areas you know of, or read about, things that you feel very deeply about.

Its not that we want you to ignore these tragedies or war atrocities, but we ask that you don't become part of that darkness. We ask that you send loving thoughts, hope and healing to all the suffering and if possible the perpetrators of the atrocities, surround them in pink love.

We know this won't be easy for you to do, especially as Earth beings seem to have the necessity of having a right and wrong in their mind about all situations, which is not always the case.

So we understand how difficult it will be to send love to what you will deem to be 'wrong or evil' but we would never ask you to do anything that would harm any one or situation.

What we ask of you is all part of the Earth changing. You will not be loved less by ourselves if you cannot achieve this difficult request, but you yourselves will know it is right, when you attempt our request.

As always, our love surrounds you.

CHALLENGE 27

Change, as in all things, must start with oneself; you cannot expect peace in the world if you are not at peace with yourself.

Peace does not mean acceptance of all things and/or being a doormat. It is being open to all ideas and thoughts, adding and subtracting to your own ideas, sharing and caring with all.

You cannot insist or expect others to do what you are not doing.

Manners begin with you, in the within. It is so sad to see the lack of them, so my child, do not forget yours, do not join the many. Let your manners shine and others will wish to join you.

Yes many will say 'how simple, and if only life were so simple' but we promise you that's how simple life can be. It is human nature that has changed a simple and beautiful life, to be complicated and deceitful. We ask that you have the strength and confidence to seek the 'simple life', not only to change your life, but those around you also.

We walk with love, with you.

CHALLENGE 28

Numbers, colours, symbols, sounds and prayer, are some of the different ways of communicating, healing, of getting in touch with one's inner soul.

Ways that are scorned by some people, who maybe haven't even tried some of the varied ways to lighten their path of life.

We ask that you learn to accept all others as they are, not for what you would like them to be.
Everyone's path is different, although, in the end, going to the same place.

Please don't always take yourself so seriously. There is meant to be laughter in life. There is nothing more we like to hear than your laughter, not only with others, but kindly about yourself.

You know yourself how uplifting a smile can be from both friend or stranger, so try to understand how much more uplifting laughter is.
Communication to one another and the soul, in any shape or form, will make lives richer and happier.

Go with God.

CHALLENGE 29

Forgiveness: this seems to be a very difficult thing for you all on Earth to do, not only forgiveness of others, but also more importantly, forgiveness of self. You are a very hard taskmaster of yourself. Then at times you ignore that you may have done something the wrong way, either knowingly or unknowingly.

If you wish others to be honest with you, please then be honest with yourself. As we have said before, all things begin with self.
Look at your own actions and behaviour and if you are not completely happy with yourself, forgive yourself and aim to do things differently next time. As you learn to forgive yourself, so shall you learn to forgive others.

After all you are living in a very difficult environment, and there is only our Mother and Father God that is all perfect, and if they can love and forgive you all, then you, as part of them, should also forgive yourself, then in turn all others.

You all have to learn, and as you learn, we as always will love you.

CHALLENGE 30

Each and every one that is either reading or having this read to you, we implore you to have more confidence in yourself and also your beliefs.

May the love you feel for life and your Mother and Father God, may it not be hid away, as if it was an illness that you don't want to share with others.

Smile more; let others see your soul, your kind heart, and your strength of not being afraid to show your Spirituality.

For as you go forward, many others will be given confidence to move forward also, and shine their light. For your light and love is needed more and more each day.

Your children and your neighbour's children need to see that there are other ways to live, than what some of them see now. They require more guidance. They need to be taught more manners. They need to be shown a more loving life style that they can copy. If they don't receive these simple, yet free lessons, how will they ever know how good life can be?

Love is for all, so as you receive our love, maybe you can share it a little more. It will never run out, for the more you use it, the greater it gets.

We as always love you.

CHALLENGE 31

Friendship, such a treasured thing, but at times so confusing and hurtful. It seems you can know many people on Earth, but really trust few. Once again we ask you to not only look into yourself, but into your heart, one of your greatest senses.

Your path here on Earth is just that, 'your path here on Earth' and the one person who knows all your goodness and faults, the one person that you give the least respect and love to, the one person you least listen to, is of course yourself. Instead of looking, learning and then being honest with your self, you tend to look outward, towards all others, and then get frustrated with others, because they too are not perfect.

Our child, no one on Earth is perfect, not even you, our beloved one.

Once again, we ask that you learn to look inwards for your greatest learning, which is of self and by knowing yourself with kindness and love, you will draw the right friendship and kindness to yourself.

CHALLENGE 32

Trees through the centuries on Earth have been a barometer or diary of life for our Father and Mother God, and also for the procession of humans.

They record in their trunk all their life's history, not only what they have gone through, but the surrounding area also.

Trees are one of nature's greatest assets; they absorb toxins and cleanse the air for all people, creatures and animals to live on Earth.

But as you and many others know, things are becoming increasingly difficult on Earth for this cleansing to continue. Many forests and single trees are disappearing and your Earth is not being cleaned as it should be, so many deeds need to be done to counter this grave problem.

We ask that you all look within your selves, to see if you can help this fragile Earth. Nothing will be too small an effort. Maybe don't throw a cigarette butt or any sweet paper through the car window, turn off the light if not needed. If you are warm, turn the heating down; don't leave the tap running if you are not using the water. If you all work together, you will be amazed how this will help your Earth.

We ask that you help us to help you. Go with our love.

CHALLENGE 33

Beauty is often said to be 'only skin deep' and 'beauty is only in the eye of the beholder' - another of your sayings on Earth, and yet more and more of you on Earth are not looking deeper than the skin of others. In fact a lot of people are only looking at the skin, then turning away from that person, not willing to share even the slightest of smiles or acknowledgement.

Some people will have nothing to do with an area or even country, tying what they think they know about the area, country and people all together, and yet what most people want and wish for is the same as everyone else, and that is World Peace.

To live and work in a peaceful happy environment, but you fail to see within yourself the lack of understanding and acceptance with and for your fellow man. Please, we ask, next time you see someone of a different culture, don't show malice or have pre-conceived ideas about them; you never know, a smile may be shared; yet another barrier may be demolished.

Small steps in all areas make big changes; just try a few small steps.

We as always walk with you, with love.

CHALLENGE 34

Beloved children, wouldn't it be wonderful if all children were 'beloved' and even more wonderful, if all children knew they were 'beloved'.

What is true and wonderful is that each and every one of you on Earth is a beloved child of our Mother and Father God.

In your quest there on Earth, some of you have chosen a really difficult path (not that any path on Earth is really easy). You wanted to progress so quickly, through the most difficult of lives, which life on Earth is; you gave yourself a very heavy load, not only to carry, but also to work through.

Please remember, we are here to help you, and we only have to be asked and we will do our best to change, assist or guide you through your darkness.

You are never alone. Be still, look, listen and know for certain you are very 'Beloved'.

CHALLENGE 35

As we look down on you on Earth, we are full of hope and love. We see bright lights of love and healing being spread by all the Light workers, of which you are one.

As you grow stronger in thoughts and your beliefs grow, so shall your light in turn grow stronger.
The darkness and negativity panics at all the goodness surrounding it. Hence you have great difficulties with peace at this time there on Earth.

The time is coming for everyone to make their choice of which path they want to progress on, and it must be their OWN choice, not that of their parent, partner or children. Their own past knowledge will help them with this decision.

This will all be part of the great changes coming to your Earth.

So we ask you to stay strong, full of light, full of belief in our Lord and Mother God, and one day, we will once again be here together, at Home. Believe that as you sow, so shall you reap.

Our love and protection
are with you.

CHALLENGE 36

Laughter: how we love to hear laughter, the natural reaction to something that is good, happy and full of love. Not the laughter that is forced or that you have to look around to see who else is laughing, or feel you should laugh to be 'with it'.

There does seem to be a cruel humour around at this time, and we are not here to criticise. We wouldn't know how to, but at the same time, we do have difficulty in understanding some of your laughter.

It is when laughter lightens your soul, and makes you feel good, for that is when your soul lights up and that is what we see and the genuineness of your laughter that we hear, then we join in with you in this joy.

For we are always with you in your life and always with love for you.

CHALLENGE 37

No matter how positive you are or how much you know of your past lives, no matter how much you believe in, or where you go to when you leave Earth, there will always be times when you feel so down, or full of despair or grief or full of self doubt. Do not stay in your darkness; please ask for our help or our Mother and Father God's help.

You are in the most difficult of lives, and on an Earth that is so full of negativity and unhappiness. No matter how spiritual you are, you will not always be strong enough to walk in the Light. Indeed because you are a 'Light' person, the darkness attacks you.

Your Light is so desperately needed on your Earth. We beg of you to ask for our help, so we may assist in cleansing and healing your aura, for your soul will never be damaged here on Earth.

Our love surrounds you, now and forever.

CHALLENGE 38

Our beloved Light beings, please do not worry as much as you do, not only about your own life, but those close to you and those in power and the media.

Every single person on your Earth has their own path to lead and one day they will have to answer for themselves on what they have done, just as you, our beloved one, will have to do. And you will only be able to tell the truth, and not move it around to include others. Yes, as we have said before, it is good to support and care for others, but not at the cost or excuse of yourself.

Your first duty, first loving, first caring, first supporting, first learning, first healing, is all with and for yourself. By doing these things for your self first, it will follow and be much easier to help others, while of course, they are learning all these things for themselves as well.

If you take care of all things for other people, you will eventually make life much more difficult, not only for them, but yourself also. You are your own responsibility; even lost souls have to learn that.

Progression comes in all speeds, but none as fast as our love to you.

CHALLENGE 39

Behold, you are all surrounded by beauty. Unfortunately you do not have your eyes open to that. There is much beautiful music in the world. Unfortunately for some, their ears are not listening to that.

Your world with all its negativity is manipulating all of your senses. Your senses belong to you and you should not be allowing television, magazines, newspapers and gossip to be manipulating you. Start questioning all you hear, all you see, all you feel.

Help your world to survive in love, fairness and the truth, not made up 'truth', which is mainly for money and the control of 'you'.

Take your own power back, gently but firmly, think for your self, do not wallow in darkness, look for the light, love and beauty. It isn't just around you, it's within you also, waiting to be unlocked and let free to grow, then to share with all your fellow beings, who are starting to do the same.

Be part of this whole new beautiful world.

As you are part of Mother and Father God, we are part of you. Go forward with our love.

CHALLENGE 40

A feather dances on the breeze; a butterfly flutters from flower to flower; a bird sings in the trees; all trying to attract your attention. There is so much love and beauty around you, but you neither see nor hear many of these things. Pressure of work, family, friends, politics and world events, all seem to take priority, and yes all these things are important at this time in your life, but not the most important.

We ask that you try and find a balance in all things. You are a unique and special individual person, as each and every one of you is, and to neglect yourself in any small way is a sin. Finding as many excuses as possible will not make it right either.

There is a saying on Earth, 'one day at a time'. We ask that you try 'one minute at a time'. We understand how hard it is to change, so don't set your target too high on anything you want to change.

Start by giving a minute a day to yourself, working up to a minute an hour. Soon that could become a half hour a day, and that in turn could be your most precious time in the day.

Just as precious as you are to us. Our love surrounds you.

CHALLENGE 41

Our beloved child, we hear your prayers. Not one word that you utter do we ignore, but we cannot always act on your request. Some times what you ask for interferes with your life plan, or some times it may interfere with someone else's life plan.

We always do what we can to assist you through your difficulties. Sometimes we try and show you a different path, but you don't always want to see or hear a different solution, other than the one you have decided on.

Can we ask that you be more open to all ideas, thoughts and solutions that are available, not only from us, but from within yourself, from life, from all around you? Just look, listen, be quiet, be open, be full of love for what you ask and somehow or other, it will be given.

For there is nothing that gives us greater joy than to help you.
For you are our greatest love. Please never forget that.

CHALLENGE 42

As we watch you struggle with darkness, not only with the darkness around you, but within also, our hearts go out to you. You are such a bright light within much darkness. It is only logical that you will attract more darkness and adversity than maybe others attract.

We ask that you try not to dwell on it. Do not give it food and nourishment to grow. It does not deserve too much of your attention. Look to us and Light for help, which will be given. For then we will nourish your Light and thoughts, working on the goodness which is in and around you, which is growing and as it grows, it will become stronger and stronger. Then that in turn will suffocate the darkness around you.

Unfortunately, this is something you will have to work on constantly, but as you do so, it will become easier, and you will learn so much by it. Your learning is staggering, and we promise you will not regret one thing.

Feel our love and protection around you.

CHALLENGE 43

As a bird soars on the thermals, over land and sea, through hills and mountains, their flight looks effortless. Nobody seems to be around to watch them fighting through wind and storms, and this, our children, is how you at times look at other people's lives, how they seem to achieve or receive what you would like, and it seems without effort on their part.

We would like to reassure each and every one of you, that the path you are on is the right one. What may be happening, as difficult as it may seem, at this time, is the right thing. You are all learning at different levels and at different depths for your future and also your Mother and Father God.

Each of you in your turn will soar on the thermals and the more you relax with life, the fewer storms there will be. You will be able to cope with life and the storms that are in your life.

Please remember, if you do feel life is too difficult, we are always with you. Just be open to our love and comfort, which we try to surround you with.

CHALLENGE 44

Life moves forward, and it seems to you all to be moving even quicker than ever. Even the young people seem to be saying that now.

There seems to be an urgency within you all, looking for answers about life, which in turn gives more questions to ask.

SO WE ASK NOW THAT YOU LOOK WITHIN YOUR SELF, WITH THESE QUESTIONS OF YOURS, AND DON'T BE AFRAID OF WHAT YOU FEEL, HEAR OR SEE. It is not to say that the academics or scientists amongst you are wrong about life. They are very clever people, but not about the heart and soul.

None of you were allowed to bring your 'home' knowledge here to Earth with you, but because of the changing energies, a fraction of knowledge of 'home' and past lives is being awoken. Do not be afraid; be happy, for you will discover how much love surrounds you.

We hope this will inspire you to be kinder and more understanding of life and of your fellow man here on Earth, and although some will be comforted, others may feel more frightened and aggressive. We ask that you should not be disturbed, but stand firm in your new beliefs and knowledge.

As we always stand by you with our love.

CHALLENGE 45

You believe……then you doubt……..and then ask
questions of yourself.
Does it really matter if you believe or not? And as you ask
yourself, you get your own reply, but for those that want it
in black and white, we will try and answer you.

You chose to come to Earth, the hardest school of learning
in the Universe. You chose your own path. You were helped
and assisted with this, and there isn't one exception among
you that wasn't urged not to try and achieve so much, in this
one of your last lives on Earth.

So now if you find it all too much, just stand back and rest
awhile. You have achieved so much by being here on Earth,
managing to work in and with the Light. You have so much
to be proud of, and after you rest, you will want to continue,
with your own questions answered.

Do not look for faults. Do not feel guilty about you and your
doubts. You're on a very difficult path, and in the end, all
will be well.

Our love always surrounds you, whatever and however you
are feeling.

CHALLENGE 46

The Power and the Glory...this as you know, is
part of a prayer that is known to almost every
one, but it can also describe an incredible view,
or describe a person that has made a lasting
impression on you.

It could also be each and every one of you.

You all have an unearthed Power within you, to
heal, to love, to learn. Also there is much
compassion to be unearthed.

There will be a day soon, when you learn to
unlock some of your power within.

As for the Glory....Each and every one of you is
made in the Glory of God. He and our Mother
God are in each and every one of you.

So we ask that you always be kinder, more loving
and more respectful to your self than you have in
the past. After all, being made in the Glory of
your Mother and Father God is indeed a
privilege.

This is one of the many reasons we walk with
you, to love and protect you, as you are the
'power and the glory'.

CHALLENGE 47

The world that you live in is going through great difficulty and although it appears to be very dark and negative, there are many Angelic presences around. There are very many humans that are being attuned to the light, healing and energy.

To help keep them slightly detached from all the enclosing negativity, we ask of all of you that read, listen or watch these words unfold, just give a few moments of your time to think happy, positive, loving thoughts, either about your family, a view, a loved one, a country or even the world, and as you think these thoughts, surround them in white or pink light.

This may be out of your natural comfort zone, but we ask that you just give it a try, and maybe try again tomorrow and the day after. It certainly won't harm anyone, and you will never know how much it will help all the Light workers that are working on their and your behalf.

Love is going to be the only thing that will change what is happening in your world, no matter what the cynics may say, and indeed they will have a lot to say. You do not have to argue with them. This only adds more negativity to your world.

Go about your life calmly and with love, and you will, my beloved ones, be doing the Lord's and Mother God's work here on Earth.

We are always with you, surrounding you with love.

CHALLENGE 48

It is not easy in this world to be good, kind, loving and understanding all of the time. Most of you Light beings do manage some of these things, some of the time, but it gets very difficult to do all of the things, all of the time.

Please do not waste too much time trying to analyse this situation. You are human. You are surrounded by intense negativity, from the television, the newspapers and of course the people you meet during the day.
Even members of your own family may not be along the Light path as much as yourself.

Do not think for one moment that gives open charter to behave in a dark and negative way, but for you to realize you are on a very difficult path. All that is asked of you is to do your best, and even if you cannot achieve the level of 'goodness' which you yourself would like, do not despair. When a similar situation arises again, you will have your chance to handle it better.

For it is those that feel no remorse of wrongdoing or blame others for their dark reaction that will need extra help and love.

If you do the best you can with what you have, you will continue to be a shining light.

We as always will be there to guide and help you when requested, with all your tasks there on Earth.

CHALLENGE 49

You all try to know others in your life, but we have to say, to know yourself is far more important. Look honestly at yourself, both on the outside and then the inside, know your good points, know and understand why you do certain things, why you repeat things in life that make you unhappy. Ask yourself why.

Were you conditioned as a child to do certain things, and then you just keep repeating them as time goes by? Do you blame others for what is happening in your life?

It is time to take account of yourself; not an easy thing to do. It takes courage and honesty to look at yourself this way, but by doing so, you will cleanse from within yourself negativity, dishonesty, old grudges, jealousies, memories that have been holding you back from the life you should have been living.

As each and every one of you do this courageous act, you will make your own life so much better, cleaner, healthier and happier, which in turn will do the same for those around you, which in turn will do the same for all life on Earth.

We ask that you never underestimate the simplicity of what we say and ask of you, to change the life you live in. It can and will work, if all the Light people work together. We may also add here, that no taxes or money or qualifications are required, just you yourself, to change your whole life. Of course, we, as always, will be surrounding you with love and encouragement. Please take our love and blessings.

CHALLENGE 50

Every day is the first day of the rest of your life. So whatever happened yesterday, or the year before, cannot be changed. You can wish it never happened, wish you had never said or done something, wished you could have thought of another response, or had not been in that place at that time.

But part of growing up mentally and emotionally is accepting the truth of what really happened. Look to the present, in the 'here and now' and see if things can be changed, an apology, look at the situation from a different perspective. If you can do nothing (that doesn't mean not wanting to do anything) then it's a lesson in life you must learn. Next time a similar situation comes around, try to handle it differently because, our beloved one, life on Earth is all about learning, not only for yourself, but for our Mother and Father God. These are lessons you asked to learn, and until you do, they will be repeated, time and time again.

So our beloved one, the more you look at yourself in honesty, wisdom and love, the sooner you will release much pain and hurt, that not only others have inflicted upon you, but what you yourself have inflicted on yourself and others.

You are not loved any the less for not being perfect. You wouldn't be on Earth if you were perfect, but you will be loved and respected more for learning, loving and correcting all in life that you can.

That means your best effort, no one else's. For you are all unique and special, and very much loved by us all.

CHALLENGE 51

Things are very confusing for you all on Earth; the world seems to be in such turmoil, as indeed it is, but not quite in the same way as you see it. There is a great power struggle. There is a great political struggle and a great monetary struggle, all going on and nothing is as it seems.

We have to say that to join or actually try and fight any of these subjects will not help to change or influence the actual outcome. It is darkness fighting darkness, trying to hide behind and influence the lighter souls, as indeed in part it has.

What we request from all that read or hear these words is what we try to say in all our messages to you. Send light and love to all people, all situations, all politicians and countries that YOU know are suffering.

We also know that this will not be easy for you to do, as a great many things we mention are dear to your own heart, and understandably hurt you and yours. So although we know it will be difficult for you to do, we still ask that you attempt to send love, light and healing to any person, situation or country that needs to change. You don't have to say what outcome you would like; just send love, light and healing.

You cannot comprehend what a difference this will make, and the more people that attempt this, the quicker a more peaceful solution will be found.

We give thanks. We love and cherish you.

CHALLENGE 52

Learning, teaching, counselling, knowledge, all wonderful gifts for any one to have. Would you be surprised if we told you that you all have these gifts and attributes?

Learning: that is the main reason you are here on Earth, to learn and grow with learning; you are never too old, never not bright enough to learn. Each and every one of you has your own pace of learning, which is right for you.

Teaching: it is for you to share your learning, but in such a way that it is a gift you give to others, just as those give you their gifts of what they have learnt.

Counselling: to be a counsellor, to friend or stranger, is one of your greatest gifts, to walk with some one, hear their troubles, to be non judgmental, offering suggestions, never stating what is best for them, only helping 'them' to find the best solution for themselves. To walk with them when they feel lonely or afraid.

Knowledge: to look, observe and register what you see, hear and read, to find the truth within all these things, in order to help you and others on the path of life.

These four things you probably never think of. Yet it is something you do throughout your life, and if given more thought and recognition, will help to change your life and others here on Earth greatly.

Our love as always surrounds and holds you.

CHALLENGE 53

Joy, Love, Healing and Wisdom are wished to all that are reading or listening to these words. And we know that as you listen and read these words, some of you will have grave doubts that what you are reading can be true, that you can be loved or even liked. You fill yourself with so much pain and sorrow with what is happening in your world, you don't think you have a right to be anything but unhappy.

We say to you, that is not the reason you were allowed to come to Earth. Your own path is difficult enough. You took a lot on board, to learn to challenge yourself with. Yes it is good to help and support others. To be caring is one of your wonderful traits, but as your problems are yours, so do others have their own problems to tackle, and it is the wisdom that you learn in life progression that you should be learning from, which problem to help others with and how far to help, and which to leave for others to sort out.

Your life, no matter how many challenges you applied for, always leaves room for joy and love. Step back, and see yourself as you really are, and ask if you are neglecting yourself for others. It could also be if you concentrate on others you don't have time to look at yourself honestly.

The time is now, to see, feel and hear what is meant for you, and in doing so you will be able to spread more love, joy, healing and wisdom to all that you meet on life's path.

As we try to pass our joy to you and surround you in love.

CHALLENGE 54

Your heart, soul and belief are very much like the tides of the oceans. They come and go with belief and knowledge. Do not worry little one; this is how it is to be at the moment.

As the energies clear, so will you see your path of life more clearly. You do well, all of you, to love, help and work not only for your own progression, but others as well.
You are all living in a very complicated time of unrest and negativity, but you, others and we are working so hard to change life on Earth, for each one to be more kindly, more understanding, more accepting and loving to all your fellow men.

Of course there are many entities that do not wish for this to happen. Power and control are great evils in man, and are often wrapped up in so-called goodness and religion.

The pure love that our Mother and Father God are and the love they have for all of you. Accept that their children (who you all are) have to find their way through all sorts of problems, but life was never meant to be all good or all bad, but we trust and know you will all return home more knowledgeable, more loving and more understanding of all, and your wisdom will surely help all others.

You are very much respected and loved by us all.

CHALLENGE 55

Healing seems to be a misinterpreted and misunderstood word in your language. Yes, a bone in your body can be repaired, an illness can disappear for a while, but our healing doesn't necessarily mean curing and waving a magic wand, and all you don't need goes away.

A lot of things need to happen to a person or situation before they or it are healed.
If darkness can be removed from within, and fear can be dissolved, if we can remove a lot of unnecessary worry from your minds, then light and love can move into the person or situation, to show everything in a different light. You come to know yourself better. You begin to understand so much more about your life. You start to look at all things from a different perspective.

Move with the change; give thanks; enjoy the moment. Then you will not only have the effect of 'healing' in the here and now, but so many layers of healing may take place, so it becomes an ongoing healing.

Through all this, we will walk with you and help as much as we can, without interfering with your life plan. For you are our joy and love.

CHALLENGE 56

In your very busy lives that you all seem to live these days, full of things you feel 'must' be done, not only for yourselves, but for others also, we ask that you take a step back, have a few moments for yourself, have a picture in your mind or a view on a post card, that brings you a sense of love for its beauty. Some of you may not need the help of a picture, but others, because your minds are so full of what you are doing that day, will find it helps you to get to your quietness within so much quicker.

In time, this period will become more and more important to you, a special part of your day, which will help you cope and sort out problems you were struggling with. A lot of the time you struggle with problems that are not even yours, and while you worry about them, they are more than likely being ignored by those they belong to.

It is time for you ALL to take responsibility for yourself, and move forward in your life. We will always be there to help not only you, but all others also.

For our love for you has no boundaries.

CHALLENGE 57

We ask that all that are on the Light path of healing, searching for truth, reading words of love and spirituality, we don't just ask, we implore you to have more confidence not only in yourself and your own beliefs, but to gently bring these things into conversation with those that you meet. We don't mean having a banner or shouting from hill tops, but gently and firmly, own what you say and think in your spiritual knowledge.

Do not be afraid of being ridiculed. Do not be afraid of being laughed at, or spoken about behind your back. You will be surprised how many people are beginning to think like yourself, and if not, it will set a seed in their heart, to grow, and them to think.

Time is short, and you need to show your allegiance. You need to show others on the same path, that they are not alone, and as the number of people grow in honesty, so shall all your strength get greater and greater, and your knowledge become stronger.

Even as we speak, we can see you grow in confidence. Please remember, we are just a few of those that love you, and walk with you, so never be afraid.

Love and Honesty should never be afraid, and if you are, call for us to come to your assistance, for we are always there for you, with love and protection.

CHALLENGE 58

What a learning curve each and every one of you are on, and for the many different things to be learnt, so there are as many different reactions from each and every one of you. Even when your self is given the same problem as previously, but with distance in-between, you react so differently from the time before. Sometimes it's with wisdom added; sometimes your reaction is different, just because of the mood you are in.

The point of telling you these things now is that the time has come for you not to be critical of your fellow man. They may not be doing things the way you would like things or matters done and sorted, but like you, they are on their path of life and trying the best they can to move forward and learn.

Not only do we ask you not to be critical of others, but yourself also. So much energy is spent on criticism and self-criticism. Replace that with love and helpfulness, and by doing so, you will allow yourself and others to move forward so much quicker.

If your help or knowledge is asked for by others, then by all means please help, otherwise, concentrate on your learning, which in turn, won't be just for yourself, but others also.

Your Earth life will change so much quicker also, and become the place of much happiness, not only for yourself, but your children and your children's children.

As we regard you as our children, we try to protect and nourish you, and of course love you unconditionally.

CHALLENGE 59

Your own truth and honesty are so important. When we say 'your own', we mean all you have learnt from reading, listening to or seeing with your own eyes, then you take from that all that relates and resounds true to you yourself. Do not accept someone else's truth, information or learning, without first questioning and studying it from all directions. From that which you have learnt will come your own truth and honesty.

The next bit becomes a little more difficult, because then you have to walk, talk and own your own truth and honesty, and that may not be the same as what is believed by those around you at the time.

It doesn't necessarily mean that their truth is wrong; it just doesn't belong to you. So don't be brow beaten into believing others more than yourself, nor should you stick to your guns for the sake of being stubborn. If you wish to 'tweak' or change your truth and honesty, that is fine also, for as you learn and grow, all changes. Just be sure they are your changes, and not someone else's.

We love and cherish you, whatever you say or think, but like all protectors, we just want the very best in every respect for you, our beloved child.

CHALLENGE 60

War never has and never will solve any of the world's problems. It may seem that it does, as fear can rule, as can hunger. People can be left with so little self-esteem; they lose faith, not only in themselves, but the country and world they live in. But rest assured this is only a temporary existence, not only for the <u>so-called</u> winners, but the <u>so-called</u> losers as well.

Most of you have had experience of both sides of this problem. Through your own choice, you have felt there was such a need to learn and experience the depth of despair as well as the elation of being a 'winner'. Now you know all these feelings and want to do all in your power to change things in the here and now, which indeed you can, and are doing.

So we ask that you continue, firstly to be at peace with your self and full of love, then to send this outwards. If you feel you cannot do this, as it feels too strange, start by aiming this love, hope and peace to the television, the radio or pictures in the newspapers, to wherever you are feeling, seeing or hearing what disturbs you. We promise this will and is making a big difference to your life on Earth.

We promise that we never leave your side; we are but a whisper away, as indeed our love for you is always surrounding you.

CHALLENGE 61

Seconds, minutes, and hours, followed by days, months and years, measure time on your Earth. This seems to make understanding of time that much easier for you.

It is only Earth that has such 'timing,' so we ourselves do not always find it easy to understand your need to know 'when' and how much you rely on timing.

By being obsessed or reliant on timing, we wish to point out that you miss so much life and beauty. Because of not living in the minute or day and looking ahead of the present time, you miss the sunshine, the birds singing and you forget to smell the flowers. You seldom think about your wonderful memories.

We do understand that when you are going through a particularly bad patch in life, you may not want to live in the 'day' but just dream of a better part of life, further ahead in time, but if we can persuade you to take each day at a time and a little slower, we promise you there will be something in that day that will bring a little smile to your lips, and gladden your heart with love, if only for a little while.

It breaks our hearts when you are so sad and unhappy, so if only for a second or minute, just be still and feel our love surround you, and believe us when we say, our love for you is and always will be with you.

CHALLENGE 62

Some of you reading or listening to these words at this moment in time will be wondering, how come? This isn't in the usual scope of your interest. You didn't mean to be here, or reading these words. It just happened

Well my beloved one, I have to tell you that this is happening to so many people right now. The awakening to new and moving energy, the search for Peace, Love and Healing, not only for oneself, but the whole world, is finding such a strong momentum, that many people are getting swept into the spiritual love without realizing it.

Please do not be afraid. No one in these writings wants to control you, hurt you or charge you a fortune in money. All we will have done and will ever do is love you unconditionally, protect you and guide you, when you allow us, to tell you the truth when you ask, and as your life on Earth is changing, attempt to guide you to a more peaceful, loving, nonviolent environment. We wish to hear the merry sound of your laughter, instead of the anguish of your tears.

As more and more people join your inquisitiveness, and your search for truth, (which in your heart and soul you have always known), the momentum will get stronger, and you will all move forward so quickly, to a brighter, more loving and peaceful world.

We are only sorry that you are going through such pain and unhappiness on your Earth at this time, but we ask that you stay strong, loving and full of light, for the coming and wonderful new life, that is for all people.
We are beside you, and always will be, loving you unconditionally.

CHALLENGE 63

Our ABC..... To you all

Angel	We always surround you
Beautiful	You always are in our eyes
Caring	As we care for you, we ask you care for others
Divine	The Divine presence is always around you
Energy	Is changing, as you are
Faith	Is within, just be open to it
God	You are His/Her child
Heaven	Is Home
Inner	All is within you
Joy	Is what you are wished
Kindness	Show to your self
Love	Send Love, Receive Love, Share Love
Mother	Always watches over you
Nativity	You were all born into this world
Observe	See more with your eyes
Perfection	Only exists at home
Quality	Is in the eye of the beholder
Reassurance	Is given to you, whenever you ask
Steadfast	Stand firm in your belief
Truth	Always use Your truth
Understanding	Not only of others, but of yourself
Vertical	Always reach up, there will be Light
Wings	You can fly with us

X	Is a kiss
You	Are so important
Zen	The truth, in one's heart

We present you with a new alphabet. We send you all the above, so you may live your life more lovingly and more peacefully, and with Grace.

CHALLENGE 64

You all, at times, sit and reflect on what has gone from your life, be it loved ones, friends or even places. By saying that which has gone, we don't necessary mean through death, although it could be. It could be by moving home, moving to a new area, maybe a new country to work. It could be through 'life', its self-changing course. You may lose touch with those that have meant a lot to you at the 'right time'. It is not always possible to keep contact with all people in your life, even if they meant something special to you, as indeed, there will be people whose life you have touched and you may never know how much.

What we ask, as you sit and remember, always try to remember the good things. Don't waste your wonderful energy on recalling things that went wrong, the arguments you may have had. For believe us when we say no one returns home carrying resentment, or harbours any hate for people still remaining on Earth.

The only person that has to forgive is you yourself. You have to forgive yourself for all that has taken place, learn from it, and when a similar situation arises, aim to handle things better or differently. For, our beloved children, the reason you chose to come to Earth, the hardest planet in the Universe, was to learn, and not necessarily as an academic, but with matters of the heart and wisdom.

Be kind with yourself, with your reflections, for you are very much loved.

CHALLENGE 65

The days grow shorter, the air warmer, the energy more confusing. Do not be afraid, our loved ones. This is all meant to be; the changing of all your lives, the only thing that is not known is how each and every one will react to these changes. There will be those that are afraid, and we ask that you remain calm within, and trust in your own instincts.

There will be those that want more power and control (which is happening all over the world) not just for themselves, but also over others too. We have to give you the understanding that the power and control of yourself belongs to you alone, and no one else. We ask that you state this to yourself and believe it. You do not have to fight or argue with anyone about this. Just state it as the truth, and when all people learn to do this, softly, gently, but with certainty, then it will be so.

Nothing has ever been solved by war and destruction, not on a permanent basis, only temporarily. The same is with anger, or saying unkind things about someone, along with gossip. The time has come to be kinder, more loving to yourself and others, and when that is not possible, just send light and love to the person or situation; and let go; don't harbour negativity about the situation.

We are with you, giving you this strength and love; call for more help if you feel what you are receiving is not enough. We remain with you, surrounding you with love.

CHALLENGE 66

Love and Truth: the two most important things here on your Earth. Not money, not work position, nor your family position.

Love doesn't mean to go around freely giving of yourself, but doing the best you can, not only for others, but yourself also. Being kind, considerate, respectful, to each and every one, including yourself, all these things and more add up to Love.

As for Truth, your truth may not be the same as others, but we ask that you always try to live your truth. Following these two seemingly simple rules will raise you to a new awakening and energy, will lift you further than you ever imagine you could attain in your awareness of life here on Earth.

In this time of great change, many things that you will not understand are happening all around you. Please remember, that each and every one of you is on your own path, and as much as you may care and love someone, they have their own path to walk, and if things are not as you would dream them to be, please remain strong, not only in your belief of life, but in all those you love.

We are here with you and our love, and although we may not always be seen, we can be sensed and felt, any time you are quiet and centred. There should never be any doubt, for this is our Truth. We are always with you.

CHALLENGE 67

When darkness and confusion surround you....sometimes from out of the blue.....sometimes for a particular situation or meaning...we ask please try not to blend with these feelings.....do try to detach yourself a little from the problem(s). It is often because you are so involved, that you do not see the truth or solutions to your pain.

Others often want to interfere with your life because they think they know your answers. That of course is not true. Only you yourself know what is right for you, and by just stepping back a little from the situation, things will become much clearer to you, and as time moves forward, you will learn to do this more often, and like all things, the more you do your own solution solving, the more life will become clearer, brighter, stronger and more loving.

Shake off the negativity that surrounds you, and if it still tries to enter your very being and you feel you cannot cope, ask us for protection. We will always answer you as you call, for you are our only concern and love. We never leave you, but cannot interfere or help unless requested to do so.

Just whisper, we hear you in our sleep. Our love surrounds you.

CHALLENGE 68

Read, look and listen.
Read all kinds of books, magazines, and leaflets. Open up your mind to all new learning. But be sure to put your own interpretation on all things that you read. Take what belongs to your own knowledge, your own understanding of life. Read between the lines. See if it is the truth, or do they want to control your thoughts? Be responsible for all you learn and pass on to others. After all, knowledge is for all to share.

Look, not just at a situation, object, person or place, but all around it or them. See if goodness, love and light are also present. If not, why not? Do you need to be around that particular situation, object, person or place? Can you input goodness, love and light? If you can, then please do so. If not, just send love to the situation, object, person or place, then move to where you would feel more comfortable.

Listen, not only to others, but to yourself also. Do not just hear the words you want to hear, but listen carefully to what is being said and not said. You all, at times, speak too quickly and hurt others unintentionally, as indeed do others to you. You sometimes guess what others are saying or trying to say. Don't guess, ask. If you always give your truth to others, in time they will give theirs to you. If you find that they don't, then think carefully, do you need them in your life?

Be responsible for all you read, look at and listen to. Cleanse your life and inner self of all negativity. As you all try to achieve this, we will hold you in our hearts and minds to assist and help you. For you always have our love and strength.

CHALLENGE 69

Kindness comes in all shapes and sizes. At times you give kindness to others without realizing that is what you are doing. Your manners and way of life are such, that treating some other human beings with courtesy you would expect from others, can be an eye opener for them.

There are a lot of souls on Earth that do not get offered kindness in their lives at all, and yet some of you on Earth seem to expect these people to be kind and loving, expect them to behave without malice and discourtesy. That would be almost impossible for them to behave that way.

We do not aim to make excuses for these people, only offer understanding. We would ask, if possible, that you look a little deeper than what you actually see, and if possible treat each human being with the same respect as you would like to receive.

We are not asking that you go out and change the whole world, but we assure you that by showing a fraction more kindness than you usually do, people and situations will begin to change very quickly. So many people are already on this path, and great changes are being made, Please join the 'kindness club'.

We walk with you always. With our love and your kindness, your life will be so much happier.

CHALLENGE 70

When you are on the Spiritual path, there only ever seems to be questions. For as soon as you get one answer it seems to move you on to the next question, all the time leading you down a path of magical wonders, or would be wonders, if you slowed down, just a little, and didn't try to absorb all other things too.

There seems to be a great urgency to get from A to B, so much to do in one day, so many things to absorb, listening to the radio, seeing television, reading books, collecting a mound of information off the internet, filling yourself up with a great deal of negativity and information that you may never need, filling yourself up with problems that hurt and worry you, thinking that you cannot change anything.

Please, just slow down a little, find your own quiet space, somewhere you feel safe, and preferably on your own. Contemplate all that worries you this day, and listen carefully to the small voice within that is always there to help and assist you. Trust your inner wisdom, for it is this connection that will give you all the answers that you will ever need in life. It will be the truth; it will be surrounded by love; and it will never hurt anyone. And that, my precious one, is how you will know that it is from the voice within, and not from the negativity that surrounds you.

If ever you are not sure of anything, just ask. We will, wherever possible, help you, without taking away your own free will. For we are always with you, as is our love for you.

CHALLENGE 71

Place your trust in what your heart feels to be right, in all
that you hear, see or feel, be that through word of mouth
from a friend, work colleague, television, radio, newspaper
or magazine. Follow your own truth; do not be led by
someone else's word.

It is not through lack of trust of others that we request this of
you, but we wish you to learn and believe in yourself, for all
that you will ever need to know, to help you through this life
of yours, is within. You have the key to unlock all your own
answers, and as the energy changes on Earth, you will find
more and more information comes from within.

Have courage, our beloved one, to hold steady in your light
and belief, not through anger, but love. You don't have to
convince any others, for they will see your truth, as you will
learn to see their truth, and all of you will help to bring forth
a different way of life on your Earth, a much more loving,
understanding, accepting, sharing, caring world, for you all
to work together for the Earth and mankind.

And as you walk your path, please remember, we are but a
whisper away, and our love for you even closer.

CHALLENGE 72

All you children of light who are reading or listening to these words, we ask that you do not feel confused, because we call you children.

On your Earth, a child is young and learning. They then move on to youth, then teenager, before becoming an adult. But to us here at home, you are all our children, children of our Lord and Mother God, and although you have advanced so much on the Earth plane, even through such adversity, you have learnt and progressed so much, you will to us always be classed as our children, while you are there on Earth. This is said through love, not to make you feel inferior or belittle what you are and have become.

It could also be a lesson for you all to learn. There is always something to learn, always something to have fun with, always more questions to ask, lots of working out to do, trying to understand how others get to the answers they do, when they are so different to your own.

So we hope now that it has been explained a little to you, that you will understand why we call you children, children of Light, so open, so inquisitive, so loving and may you always be so.

We hold your hand; we love you as our precious child, now and always.

CHALLENGE 73

Truth, your own truth in all things, is one of the first and foremost important steps for you to take in your life of development, the development of your spirit and loving nature.

We know this is not always easy, especially if you feel it could hurt or confuse someone that you have respect for. But to own your own truth and opinion is living as you need to, want to and should be living. We don't ask that you deliberately hurt others, but do not agree with them against your better judgement and thought, for this in the long run will hurt and confuse them even more. It will also confuse your inner self, for as we say many times, all is known within you, within your soul, all you are meant to be doing in this life, and lying was never on your agenda.

Keep your heart, soul and aura as clear, clean and healthy as is possible in this world of yours, where so many people are struggling in the negativity. We ask those of you with extra strength to set an example of using your own truth.

Never fear that this will do you harm, because truth, along with love, will always succeed, Then you will move further forward, up into the Light, where you belong.

We are always watching and cherishing you, with your beauty of heart, and your need to do right, not only for yourself, but others also. We walk with you and love you always.

CHALLENGE 74

You have been told many times that the only person that restricts you from doing anything in your life is yourself. And although this is very true, we can see how, at times, you feel it is not possible that you can change, or do things differently in your life.

We would like to highlight some of the most common reasons for lack of change and ask you to look and see if any of the following belongs to you, and if so, how it may be possible to change and move on.

You may be controlled by thought or deed of someone close to you. Why should they want to do this, if not for their own power? Each and every one of you is our Lord and Mother God's child, who asked to come to Earth. Do not give away one of your greatest gifts, and that is one of free will. Use it wisely, and travel far on life's path.

You could be controlled by the state or country you live in. You could be living in fear of expressing what you want or need in life. This is being controlled by a few who also want power and control; but there is no greater power than being a quiet, honest, hard working, clean living person, who only wants the greater good of all and to harm none. There are more of you wanting the same thing than you give credit for. Speak quietly, and not in anger, to your neighbour and friends, and you will be able to change the world.

Maybe you do not have the confidence or self belief for going forward in life, to meet new challenges and enjoyment. Somewhere along the path of life, you have allowed this to be taken from you or you have even given it to some one, in the belief that they know more than you.

We ask that you now awaken to a new day, a day that belongs to you, to take responsibility for yourself. We ask you to believe us when we say: you can do anything, be anything on this Earth. All we ask is whatever you choose, may it be not only for the greater good of yourself, but all others also, and to harm none.

Do not be afraid, for we as always walk with you, with love and protection.

CHALLENGE 75

To know, to love, to understand others in your life is not easy. All too often you, on Earth, jump to conclusions about others.

You so wish to meet and be with someone that reminds you of 'home', someone that loves, cares and has unconditional regard for you, that most of the time you only 'glimpse' at the person or people you are meeting. Then you add your own wishes or presumptions to who you are seeing.

What we ask of you all is to practise on yourself, to see yourself honestly, along with understanding and loving of yourself. Always be honest about yourself, but never brutal. By doing these things, you will have greater understanding and positive regard of yourself, which, in turn, will enable you to know and understand others to a much greater degree.

We ask you all these things, not to lecture or control, but because of our deep love of you, when you are hurt, so are we. Life is so difficult on Earth, negativity grows so strong, that we wish to help, protect and guide you, which in turn will enable you to help others. Then the light of you all will show the way, as it does in so many places already.

Walk in our light and love, for we are always there for you.

CHALLENGE 76

When life seems particularly difficult for you, which it is for all at times, and you think things are not going to change, or cannot see a way of changing your circumstances, please do not despair. Don't let your mind or imagination control your own thoughts. Don't let negativity rule you; try not to think things are worse than they actually are.

There is always light in any given situation. Maybe you cannot always see this, or maybe not as soon as you would like to.
It could be because you are concentrating on the 'bad, dark and negative' part of things or situations. You could be missing the solution by not concentrating on the light or positive side of things; therefore you keep yourself in despair longer than necessary.

Life is such a mixture of all emotions and challenges, which if you only knew, you yourself have a much greater degree of control than you actually believe.

By looking at the situation from a slightly different angle, by looking within yourself, to see how you could change your attitude, these things alone will begin to change your despair.

The one thing you have to remember, you are never alone in anything here on Earth. We are always with you, with our love and support, and even when you don't want to know or believe in us, we never, never give up on you, for our love is always with you. Always.

CHALLENGE 77

Angelic messages are not just for those of the Christian Faith, but also for each and every one on planet Earth that feels these words to be true. For each and every one on Earth is born with a Guardian Angel, who remains with them through all their life there on Earth.

To us, and of course to our Lord and Mother God, each and every one of you is special. Each one of you has your own Guardian Angel, and each of you has your own path to walk. The greatest gift you are all given here on Earth is one of choice, of your own free will.

We already hear some of you shouting that this is not so. But we promise you, it is.

You may have chosen a particularly difficult path. You may be happier conforming to other people's rules, their direction, and their way of life. It maybe is the path you want to travel, or it could be that it is just easier for you.

What we ask of you is that you be true to yourself, that you look inwards, and confirm to yourself, that what you are doing in life is what you feel is right and good for you. All the questions that you need to ask yourself are waiting to be answered from within; everything you ever need to know can be answered from within. You just need to learn how to be quiet, still and listen, which is not easy, in your busy, hectic, troubled Earth. Once again we promise it can be done, as many, many others have and are discovering for themselves.

You are not walking your path alone; we, as always, are with you, loving and encouraging you to be you.

CHALLENGE 78

When undecided about a feeling, request, project, situation or person, try not to rush your decision. Take your time, and say you will get back to the person, situation, project or request. For if it is the right thing to go ahead with or comment on, you will indeed know. If you are unsure, it may not be that it is wrong; it just may be a little out of synch. It may need tweaking at the edges. It may need to be looked at from a different angle, or indeed, it may be wrong for you.

Be it right or wrong, no true decision needs to be made in a second. This, once again, is a lesson in self-belief, by learning about yourself; this carries on to life and situations all around you.

We say this many times, for it is true. All learning, love, truth and honesty begin within. Walk your path diligently, your path not someone else's. Do not be controlled or controlling. To support others and assist, when asked, is love. To take it further may be controlling, which could take you off your path of life, and also off their path of life.

There is much to be said on the subject of control, but just by us planting a seed, you may now start to understand certain situations that are happening around you right now. Just send love to dissolve the controlling strings, which could be your own, or someone else's.

Do not be afraid. We will help, when requested, to give you strength and love, for YOU to be YOU. For we are always with you, as is our unconditional love.

CHALLENGE 79

Open up your heart. Try not to judge others, for you may or may not know, each and every one of you here on Earth is here to learn. Some have chosen a more difficult path than others. Some have even chosen the dark side of life to learn, and in time this will help them and others to put their life on a better, lighter, brighter future.

Life is not easy for any one of you, so to spend your time and energy judging others is such a complete waste of time, and of course while you are doing that, you are ignoring your own path, life and mistakes. For not one person there on Earth is perfect. There is always something that you can be doing to help yourself in life, which in turn, as always…helps others.

We say this to enable you to move quicker towards your light and true path.

These words of judging others may not be for you, but someone that is very dear to you, so we would ask that you don't 'row in' with your friend in this matter. Not that we would ask that you take them to task either. Just in your own quiet time, send love and light to the situation that was spoken about. That's all. No whys or wherefores; just love and light. Then we, our precious child, can do the rest.

We are, we know, giving you a heavy workload, and sometimes loneliness, but we are always there to help when requested to do so.

We are always with you, supporting and loving you.

CHALLENGE 80

Kindness costs so little, but means so much. There is so much that each and every one of you can do to make life on Earth so much better, a brighter and happier place to be. Just by being kinder and not only to your family, neighbours, work colleagues, people in the street, on the bus or in a shop queue, but kinder to and about yourself also.

We repeat many times, that all you need to be or know is within yourself. By being kinder firstly to yourself, you will discover things you never knew about yourself. You all have great knowledge and compassion within, but to a lot of people there on Earth, it is hidden by all the negativity that is in your surroundings. This, of course, is not only caused by your family circumstances, but by the food and liquids that you consume, by the electric magnetic fields surrounding many of you, and by now, the air and circumstances that are changing the weather so quickly.

So at this point we would like you to appreciate yourself, how well you do to be as kind as you are, and here we are asking if you can make a little more effort to be kinder still.

We have great faith, love and understanding of you, for we know whatever we ask, you will at least attempt to do. We would like to say once again, you are never alone, and you are always loved. Life is so brief on Earth. Joy can always be found in some form or other, and kindness can lead to joy.

CHALLENGE 81

There are many paths leading to the summit, but they are all
going to the same place.

This is a wonderful saying and it can be compared to many
things in life, but belief and religion seems to be the most
apt.

Religion is one of the most controversial subjects that can be
spoken about, in any language; there are so many conflicting
ideas and beliefs. What we would ask of all that are reading
or listening at this moment in time, is to look at your own
ideas and beliefs, and ask yourself, do you feel comfortable
with all you believe in? Do you feel enriched? Do you feel
love? Do you feel compassion? Do you feel the truth
within? If the answer is "yes" to all these things, then it is
right for you.

For what we are about to say now will not sit comfortably
with everyone. For what we ask you to remember is, what
suits one person, does not necessarily suit every other
person. Each and every one of you is an individual, and as
such will not think and believe the same as others. Maybe
even in your own family you will hold different beliefs. So
how would it be possible for different people, of different
countries and cultures to believe in the same?

There is nothing wrong with that. It's all part of the
wonderful variation and cultures of your life on Earth. What
is wrong is to impose your will on others, to try and make
them think and feel the same, for this will never happen.

Anything done that doesn't involve love will never last, will
only ever be temporary. For every one was given as their
greatest gift on Earth 'your own free will'. It is yours to use
as you believe. Please use it wisely.

We are your loving friends, who always walk with you,
along with our love for you.

CHALLENGE 82

We speak to each and every one of you, to give you courage and the will to move forward in light and love.

We see how difficult it is at times for you to move forward. You so believe, and want to move forward, and then something happens in your life that makes you doubt all the work you are doing, not only for the Earth, but all upon it.

What seems to upset you could be such a small thing, just a throw away remark by someone that hasn't a clue what you are doing or achieving, or something happens on Earth that makes you wonder if what you are doing will make any impact at all on your Earth.

We wish to give you hope, love, courage and the will, not only to continue your work on Earth, but with many others that are working in the same difficult circumstances, to increase your loving work whenever possible. Nothing that you do is a waste of time, love or effort; while ever you do things for the greater good of all and to harm none, you are working to achieve the will of your Father and Mother God, lighting a path for the way of great change, for all on Earth. The harder you work, the better it will be for all on Earth.

So we beg of you, do not despair; do not take on the negativity and the disbelief of those around you. Our love surrounds you. All will be revealed to all in the future, and then you will be so happy that you had the courage to work on.

Never forget, we walk with you, always!!!

CHALLENGE 83

Peace on Earth to all men. How that saying at this present time would seem to be such a difficult achievement. Yet there are many people working hard and trying within their own lives to achieve such a challenge.

Once again, we have to say, that anything you wish to achieve in life has to begin with 'within'. If you yourself can achieve a certain peace, if you yourself can spread peace and harmony within your own environment, along with many other people, you will be surprised how quickly this can spread through life.

It is no use saying 'that's all well and good, but you know many, many other people that just wouldn't do that'. That is a cop out, blaming others for something you are not doing yourself. Once again we say you have to be responsible for your own actions. Others have to make their own decisions in their own time, and after all, there are many people out there that are in front of you, trying to achieve what seems to be the impossible.

So how about trying to have peace and harmony within your own life, living by example, not gossiping and causing pain to others? Try not to put others' wrongs to right. After all, who are you to say it's wrong? We ask that you try not only to be more understanding of others, but of yourself also. It may not all seem achievable, but we promise you many are working hard and achieving the impossible already. Are you strong enough to join them? We believe you are.

We know, love and respect you. That is why we believe anything you strive to do, you will achieve. We remain, as always, by your side, with love.

CHALLENGE 84

As the weather patterns of the world begin to change, as you are all starting to notice, so the energies of the Earth are also changing. The unrest that is on your planet seems to get greater. This is because great changes are all around, and it's very hard for most to accept.

What you would call conventional means of handling situations aren't really going to help. Bullying, dictatorship and money, they, this time, are not the answer. (It never was in the past, but many didn't perceive this.)

What is helping is… all you wonderful people trying to stay steadfast in your belief of love, light and healing, going against the grain of many people around you. Don't worry when you falter. We are with you to hold you steadfast. Your help and love are so needed, not only for others, but yourself also. Never think your light and love work in just your vicinity; they spread throughout your Earth, to places you have never even thought of. All that is ever asked of you is to do your best; your love and light will shine the way for many, and all it costs is your time and effort.

Do not be obsessed by this. Lead a full and happy life. At the same time, keep in touch with nature. It will help to sustain you. As indeed we try to sustain you as well.

You are never alone. Our love and help are always there for you. Please just ask, and it will be given.

CHALLENGE 85

The expression we use 'our Father and Mother God' may confuse certain people that are reading or listening to these words. We are not talking of two separate identities, but of the same person. Then again, when we say person, you may think of someone in the same form as yourself. This also is not so. Your maker, and indeed ours, is far beyond anything you can dream or imagine. The maker of all creation is indeed the highest of all energy that there is, full of pure love and understanding of all that is, with no exception.

There are many of you there on Earth that would wish to change many people. We wish to point out that you are not there to change others. Your main job is to change yourself, by setting an example of yourself, to yourself. You will be reaching your own heights of love and understanding.

We say this many times, but all things begin with the within. To know others you must first know yourself. You are not here to change others. Support where need be, yes, but their path is their path, and no two people on this Earth are on the same path, as every one is an individual, so every one is on their own path.

Some people look to others to control, to help, to dictate to. That way, they don't allow any time for themselves, to learn and understand themselves. Then that's maybe what they want, for it is not easy to look at yourself through honest eyes; it may appear easier to put others right, than yourself.

We ask that you ask yourself, could this be you? Or is there some one in your life like this?

Have the strength to learn about yourself, and by doing this you will be able to understand others so much better. Do not let others control your life. It is yours to learn and love with, not only for yourself, but your Father and Mother God also.

Just ask, and we will help you, for we love you also, and always walk with you.

CHALLENGE 86

The word guidance is sometimes misinterpreted; guidance is not a direction, to either receive or give, but a suggestion that may be given or received.

We, as your guiding Angels, can understand how, when offering guidance to a friend and it is not accepted, that you can be upset, but please don't be offended. All on Earth have their own gift of free will, and your friend has to learn in their own way, as it is when you yourself are offered guidance and you don't accept, though when it is this way round, you can find many reasons for not accepting, the main one being, you don't hear the words as they are intended, if you hear them at all.

We are never offended by what you say or do, for we understand you are on your own learning path there on Earth. We admire and respect what you are trying to do through great negativity and darkness. We also try and guide you, but know you cannot always hear us.

We tell you now, we are always with you; never feel alone. Our love, as always, is with you.

CHALLENGE 87

We ask that you all remember, even in the most difficult of circumstances, that you are very much loved, that you are very much cherished, and when you request, very much guided. As you read or listen to these words, the shaking of your head is seen and felt by us already, but we never, never, tell you anything but the truth.

The more you listen to yourself from within, the more you listen to your own truth, the more you respect and love yourself, without vanity. The more you believe in our great maker, the Source and the Divine, who is the all loving Mother and Father God of you all, the more you will believe in this truth that we tell you.

In these very troubled times the planet Earth is going through, we ask that you wake up to the love and truth that surrounds you, that you wake up to the reality that your life belongs to you; to help where possible others and situations, but not to take over their life and their decisions, as indeed, no one should take over yours.

The only exception that could be forgiven is those that are ill or infirm, as these people require more help and assistance, but they are still required to be given the respect of their own decisions as much as possible.

Whenever you doubt what we say about our love for you, just find space and quietness, ask for us, and we are with you, ready to embrace, to give you confidence to continue on your path of light and love.

CHALLENGE 88

Peace on your troubled Earth seems to be getting more elusive in your eyes. Peace is often asked for and wished for at Christmas, for all men. We offer you this thought, of wishing Peace for all, each and every day, once when you wake up and again when you go to sleep.

All thoughts that you work on and believe in do materialize. We are not suggesting all will be Peaceful overnight, but you will help the energies that are changing so much on your Earth. You will help light and love work with the energy of life, to be calmer and more loving.

Life on Earth is changing so dramatically and it will continue to change beyond all your recognition. By assisting in a positive way, a more beautiful way of life will emerge much more quickly.

Concentrate on the much good that surrounds you all. Not easy, but there will be a wonderful outcome for each and every one of you. You cannot lose anything at all by doing this, but your gain is unquestionable.

We love and respect you, now and always.

CHALLENGE 89

Life has been made very complicated by man. It was never meant to be, but as you all learnt more about invention, learnt about power, then when money overtook bartering, a great deal changed for man. A great deal changed for life on Earth.

The words we pass to you all seem so simplistic, and some will feel life could never be that simple. But please believe us, for we have never lied to you (and couldn't any way) that our simple words and meanings and guidance are all that is needed to change your life for the greater and better.

So the ones who are able to carry out part of what we ask, please do so, for as you do, you will want to do more. This alone will and is changing the energies of your Earth, and as it gathers more and more momentum, so more people from the four corners of the Earth will join in, and the energies will change at an even greater pace, for the greater good of all men.

As your work progresses for the good of all, so will the dark forces of life stir more and more trouble. This is their panic of them losing control. Do not fear; stand firm in your Light and our love.

We never tire of telling you how much you are loved, and that we are always with you.

CHALLENGE 90

Hope, Love and Honesty are such powerful words, such powerful tools of life. With respect added, you have the perfect mixture for a wonderful life, not only for yourself, but all others on Earth.

As always, you must start with yourself. In all these four words you must apply them to yourself first. Once you are in line with these truths, to Love and Respect yourself, to be honest with yourself, to live in Hope and not despair, you will be taken on a richer, happier path than you are now. Your life will become lighter, easier to handle, so by thought and deed alone, you will be able to pass on these wonderful tools of life to others.

You will be able to handle sadness, challenges, people and problems with far more ease. You can never be without these things, for you are here to learn, but life was never meant to be all sadness, worry and hurt. So begin today by helping yourself to a new way of life.

We are always with you to help and assist when requested to do so. We always love you….and are with you always.

CHALLENGE 91

Confidence within oneself seems, in a great many people, to be sadly lacking. Your trust in yourself and your ability, whatever your ability is for, seems to depend so much on others, when in actual fact, it should depend on you alone.

Yes it is easy to find in your mind people that are clever, brainier and more intelligent than you believe you yourself to be. They may have the ability to put words together very well.
You may listen to others that are all too ready to put you down, to mock or belittle you. You may feel you have to prove to others that you are good and kind, and that they are worthy of more kindness and understanding than you yourself are.

We are here to tell you that each and every one of you on Earth is different in all ways. Similar, yes, but not the same. Each and every one of you is on your own path, which is unique to you alone, and as such has your own gift to offer life and mankind.

The hardest person you have to live up to on Earth is yourself, and having said that, you should be kind, understanding and forgiving of yourself, when, on reflection, you haven't done things as you wish you had. But that is what learning and living is all about, and the next time a similar thing happens, you will have your opportunity to do things better.

Fear no one or situation. Time is so short there on your Earth. Just do your best, and then move on to your next challenge. Respect and love yourself, as we respect and love you, as we always have and always will.

CHALLENGE 92

Joy is a word that is not used often in this day and age, either to receive or give, which in itself can cause us great sadness, as there is much joy surrounding you all. Unfortunately, it is not seen by many of you.

So much of what you read and see via television is steeped in darkness and sadness, hurt and humiliation, and the light, joy and goodness which is there also seems to be ignored or not seen by many.

We ask you all to try an experiment. For every sad, unhappy, violent or disruptive article you either see or read, look for the equivalent of good in life, for happiness, joy and hope. It's not only all around you, but within also. It just gets hidden in all the negativity and unrest that is so strong there on Earth.

Once you make an effort to search out all the good things, you will be surprised how it will start to come naturally to you and all others. Do not restrict happiness in your life; there is much Joy all around for each and every one of you.

And as always, our love is also all around you.

CHALLENGE 93

God in his/her infinite wisdom gave you ALL the freedom of choice, and 'my O my' hasn't that through the ages caused so much joy, so much sadness and much cruelty.

But without this greatest gift, your learning there on Earth would have been much less; you would not have been so advanced in your learning. Even as we speak, we can hear people say 'What advancement? How can you call the state of our planet "advanced"?' But we can assure you, with all the negativity you have to manoeuvre through, more and more of you are learning to speak from the heart, and you are learning not to be taken in by what you read or see, and to work things out in your own heart and mind; yes you are advancing.

More Love, Light and Healing are entering Earth through your hard work, which is enabling some of the greatest energies of Angels and Spirits to once again enter into your atmosphere. The reason you feel and see so much unrest and cruelty around, is because the dark forces of negativity are also feeling the new energies and are panicking at the thought of losing their power, so are being as destructive as possible to your life on Earth.

Hold strong....hold your faith in Love... be part of the new beginning. We will support and love you, through all your own doubts, as we always have and always will.

CHALLENGE 94

To know what is right and what is wrong is within all persons, but what is right and what is wrong is not the same for all persons.

This unfortunately causes much strife and unrest, bitterness and even untimely death to persons on Earth.

After learning to accept, understand and love oneself, then it is time to move on, to do the same to all your fellow men. We understand that this is not an easy task for you all, but until you all learn to accept your fellow man, if not completely understanding him, there cannot be everlasting PEACE to you all on earth.

Time has come for this understanding to be important. Time has come for all resources to be shared. The time has come for acceptance of difference, without any particular nation gaining power over his fellow man. This should not come about by fear and war, but by the Grace of your heart.

Respect on all levels of understanding, acceptance and sharing are desperately needed for you all. As we say many times, everything begins with the within. So start right now by having respect for yourself, then you will be accorded this as your due right. As it shall be for you personally, so it will be for all persons.

Our love for you never changes; it is always with you.

CHALLENGE 95

Time…..in your mind, you always imagine that there will be time in the future to do all the things you would like to do, like reading, travelling to new places, walking, learning, art work, sport, some may feel that they would like to do voluntary work.

Always in your mind, thinking there will be plenty of time to do things……..
Some time in the future.

There should always be time in your life to do something you really want to do right now. Family is very important, work is important, but so are you, and some time each week or month, you should dedicate time to yourself. If you have a partner, they too should be allowed this time for themselves, with no jealousy involved between either of you. It doesn't necessarily have to involve cost. Life is sometimes very hard financially. There are things to do that don't involve money. It could be that you have never thought about some of the things mentioned above. We ask that you now do so. Time is also for you, and it will also be a way to understand yourself even better.

Walk with our love surrounding you.

CHALLENGE 96

How or why….hope or despair….good or bad….right or wrong….quick or lengthy. You have opposites in everything there on Earth, and never ever will anything be one sided, except maybe your own opinion. You should always try to see any situation from the opposite position, or one of the great many points in-between that a situation can be looked at. Just shifting a little in your opinion will throw such a different light on the matter.

Not only a different light will shine on the situation, but also much learning for yourself on any situation or problem you may have. To be open to new ideas and new teachings will take you faster towards the light and love of understanding, not only for yourself, but your fellow man.

When you understand your fellow man, and accept him as he is, and he you, then there will be no need for confrontation, for you both will be able to talk things and situations through. It sounds unbelievable, but we assure you it is possible. If you all work together, and the intention is for the higher and greater good of all, then anything is possible in life, even everlasting Peace.

We always offer Peace with our Love to you.

CHALLENGE 97

Respect seems to be a forgotten word in many quarters of life, and of course must be for the self first. For how can you expect anyone to respect you, if you yourself have no respect for yourself?

Once you have achieved respect for yourself, then you move on to the next stage, respecting those around you. Respect does not mean to be humble to others, as indeed you should not wish others to be humble to you.

Acceptance is a great deal of the respect we are meaning, along with kindness, and empathy. Once this is shown to yourself, it will become second nature to show this to your fellow man. And by this alone, life for all will become more meaningful and fulfilling, even by those you believe could never be kind or respectful…but they will, for they will not want to miss out on all they witness.

Sounds too simple? Life is simple; it is mankind that has made it complicated. Just try it; see if it works for you.

You are in our sights; you are ever in our Love.

CHALLENGE 98

Hear all, see all and repeat none. If only, my beloved child, you and all mankind could live more by that saying.

So many people are hurt by idle chitchat. What is strange is that a lot of people who are hurt by this chitchat do the talking as well. There is so much of interest all around you, so much love and kindness. Yet so many people think it is their right to criticise other people, or they think they know better how to run other people's lives, and simply ignoring their own character and their life.

You all have a difficult job there on Earth. If as much effort was put into managing your own life, as some of you put into other people's lives, we promise you, life would be much kinder and loving for all people on Earth.

When we offer all these suggestions, we offer them in love and kindness, to make all your lives clearer, happier and more loving. No one needs all these lessons, but all need some of them, and by putting them into writing so that you may listen to them, we are hoping to ring a bell of awareness within you, and that you may try some of these suggestions with an open mind and heart.
We are walking with you, along your difficult path, surrounding you in Love.

CHALLENGE 99

As you all on Earth go through life, sometimes full of joy, sometimes despair, please remember that you are there such a short time, although at times we know it seems such a long time to you.

It is all part of your learning, not only for yourself, but also for our beloved Maker. And the more you achieve in your heart and in your spirit and soul, the more you will advance towards your ultimate goal.

Try not to make your load heavier than it was meant to be. There is always room for lightness and a smile, if not for yourself, then someone nearby.

Darkness alone belongs to dark souls, and to be reading or listening to these words is proof you are not a dark soul.

Hold strong through all your adversity, asking for help when you feel yourself falter. This is not a weakness, but knowing your own strength and weaknesses in itself is a great strength.

We hold you near our hearts, and surround you in love, now and always.

CHALLENGE 100

Speak to others as you would like to be spoken to. Listen to others as you would wish to be listened to. Give time, love and caring and energy to as many people as possible.

We know it is not possible for you to treat everyone or even some of your own family this way, but we would ask that you treat kindly all people in this world that you can, and those that you cannot, do not wish any harm to them, just move on with your life.

For there will be a time in the near future, when kindness to all will be of the utmost importance, and if you are already in the mould of doing this, you will be already on the right path.

We know these things which we say sound so simple, but we are aware how difficult at times they are to carry out. As you try to succeed, when asked, we will help you also.

For you are our beloved, and we watch over you with love.

CHALLENGE 101

It is said that you can only 'judge others' by how you think and behave yourself, but this is not always so.

What about the times that you do judge others and your words and thoughts are not very kind about those people? Could it be what you see in others is within yourself also?

If each and every one of you could accept others for what they are, or have unconditional positive regard for them, you all would be living within much more harmony.

And already we can hear certain people say, 'That would be fine in la la land, where they don't have robbers, muggers, bullies or thugs.' We can assure you that these people are in a minority, and would be even more so, if those people that don't belong in the category of robbers etc., could think more unconditional thoughts towards people, rather than just going with the negativity and dark thoughts of these people's actions.

As we have said before, the energies are changing on Earth so quickly, that a lot of people are being more destructive. It is part of their rebellion. So it is up to you, our cherished loved ones, to work on passing on light and love wherever and to whomever you can.

We will give you strength and love to carry on and achieve even more than you do now.

We forever walk with you and love you.

A small selection of Books and People that have helped and are still helping me on my own Spiritual path. You may find some of them interesting.

The Other Side and Back	Sylvia Brown
Reiki for Life	Penelope Quest
Spiritual Growth	Sanaya Roamn
You Can Heal Your Life	Louise L. Hay
Peace Love and Healing	Bernie Siegel
Angel Therapy	Doreen Virtue
A Little Light on Spiritual Laws	Diana Cooper
Reflections – The Masters Remember	Edwin Courtney